Walking in Your Destiny, Moving Through the Fear

Compiled by Kathleen D. Mailer

Copyright © 2015

ISBN 978-1-897054-78-9

Published by: Aurora Publishing – a Division of: Doing Business God's Way International Inc.

Walking in Your Destiny, Moving Through the Fear, Compiled by Kathleen D. Mailer

The publisher gratefully acknowledges the many publishers and individuals who granted our *Walking in Your Destiny* stories permission to reprint in the cited material.

DISCLAIMER: Each author is writing from her own viewpoint and it does not necessarily reflect the viewpoint of the publisher, compiler, editor and other members of the team. It is written to inspire, motivate, and activate each heart that reads it. The reader cannot hold the publisher, compiler, editor or any other members of the team accountable for any outcomes or conclusions they come to as they read.

Walking in Your Destiny

Moving Through the Fear

Dedication

This book is dedicated to the amazing women who came to the "A Book Is Never A Book Boot Camp" in 2015.

Aurora Publishing couldn't be more proud of you for stepping up and stepping out in your destiny.

You are the first graduates to participate in this little treasure for God's glory. May this book help you go to the next level in your life, your business and your ministry!

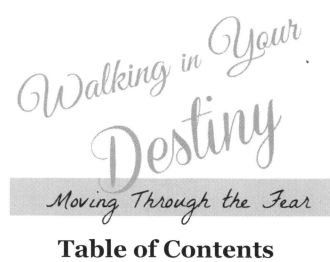

Walking in Your Destiny

Moving Through the Fear

Table of Contents

Acknowledgements

I would personally like to thank our wonderful team that work behind the scenes to help make the book boot camp unique, special, and meaningful.

Special thanks go to Dan Mailer, who is always present, always pulling together every last detail and always a pillar of strength in our events. Without your covering, these events would never have the impact they are meant to.

Coralie J. Banks, who graciously gifted us with her editing services for the purpose of this project, I thank you. Your heart to serve the Lord is inspirational. I know you were "pressed in" for the time frame (getting the book written, edited and published within 3-5 days makes it a monumental challenge). You took the challenge and you delivered. Thank you.

Another shout out must go to our good friend, Linda Olson. She believes in God getting the glory for each of our stories. Thank you for your "ear" as I prepared for the boot camp. Thank you for the support you have given us in the sharing of our message and platform. Thank you for allowing us to be a part of you and Rick's life. Together we will help international Christian authors, speakers, pastors and business leaders find their passion, package their purpose, and provide for their families. This is just as God intended it to be.

This would not be complete if I didn't acknowledge one of the most AMAZING graduating classes of the Book Boot Camp. This year was OVER the top thanks to you.

It is truly my pleasure and honor to watch each star rise to new heights.

Your inevitable success is evident within the pages of this treasure book.

Praise you Lord Jesus for giving us life and giving it in abundance. My gratitude is beyond words. I pray that my life will somehow be worship to you.

Kathleen D. Mailer

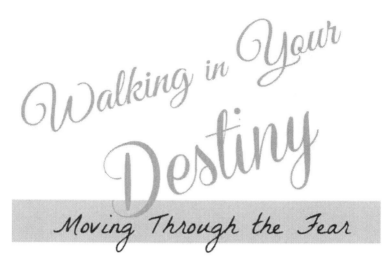

Introduction

I never want to take for granted this blessed and wonderful platform that the Lord has given both my husband and me.

I sit in awe and marvel at the work that our Lord Jesus Christ is doing in the lives of so many that He deems family.

A few years ago, I felt the Holy Spirit ask me to move our business (the Lord's business & mine) to work with Christians and help them break free of the bondage that binds them from fulfilling their destiny.

That meant I needed to:

1. **Re-brand my workshop:** *How To Write, Publish & Market Your OWN How-To Book NOW-* had to be changed to, ***A Book Is Never A Book Boot Camp.*** (It's true, ask the hundreds of our graduates who have been through the process! They will all tell you, a book is SO much more!) And, I had to reach those who have a deep passion for their message. I now had to invite only those who feel that their message is truly a ministry and who know that it is their CALLING to get that book into the hands of the people that need it.

2. **Change my language:** I talk at great lengths about this subject of Master Relationship Building in my book, *Prepare To Prosper, Taking Your Business To A HIGHER Level.* Why? Because our language is MOST important. A simple example of a language change is the fact that I no

longer call our Aurora family of authors "clients" – no... I lovingly refer to them as *Partners*. It truly IS a partnership. I feel that if you bring your gifts, talents and abilities and mesh them with mine, we can give God the Glory. With Him in the middle there is NO weapon that forms against us that will prosper! If God is for us, who can be against us? Am I right?

3. **Be obedient:** I needed to continue to listen to the words of the Holy Spirit. Read God's word. Apply God's word. Release the old "wine-skin" and let Him replace it with the new. I preach what I practice. I practice what I preach.

I feel that we all, as God's children, must always push through fear, frustration, and defeat – without holding on to pain, un-forgiveness, and past regrets.

It is out of the changes, that this book was born. The Lord is all about blessing us coming and going. This year, our boot camp was going to be even more special because it was the first year (without our graduates knowing) that we could introduce this concept of writing, publishing and marketing the *Walking in Your Destiny* book, together. As a matter of fact, it will now become a "series" and its own brand that will be a platform reserved ONLY for graduates of our Boot Camp - each and every year. Praise God!

Within the 3 Days
of the Book Boot Camp

- We had this manuscript written. The fun part is that Book Boot Camp students didn't even know that was going to happen!
- The cover was designed.
- The book was edited
- It was sent off to layout.
- We created and shared the marketing platform for everyone to use.
- We uncovered a plan for each graduate to go home and **MAKE money immediately** with **this book.** That is right. They have a book at the end of

the 3 days that they can market right away.

- They can order their copies of the book wholesale the following week and get to work creating income, making an impact and changing lives.
- Within 10-15 days, the book will be available on Amazon for retail sale – and will show them as a Co-Author.
- The most fun, was watching them become a PUBLISHED AUTHOR in a few days! What that does for a person who longs to be somebody and do something huge for Christ is incredible.

What's the great thing about God? Is the fact that this was just a "gift" from Him. It was just a side bonus of the three days. It is a physical manifestation of the components of what we taught in the 3 days.

The Boot Camp Experience

Students receive:

- The opening of their ears and hearts to the Holy Spirit's leading.
- The book(s) they are to write. (Which one to write first if they have multiple books.)
- The working title
- A complete outline of their personal book
- The *S.E.E.D*™ *Formula* that they can use time and time again to not only write books but articles, keynote speeches and more.
- The *"Next Level Thinking" Publishing Process*™ . Simply put, you need to think about your future when you decide how and what you are writing and publishing. For many authors, understanding this is what makes or breaks your sales at the end of the day.
- *Predictable Profitability*™ **Strategies.** Marketing platforms that help our authors make money even before their book is published.

- **Divine appointments** with incredible, life giving, same thinking, mission driven, Holy Spirit filled, gifted individuals from all walks of life. Many of our graduates speak of "friendships for life" coming from this event. They are encouraged to work together, give accountability to each other, pray for one another, and lift one another through the ebb and flow of the book writing process. Yes, PARTNER on some level with one another – even through marketing, social media platforms, sharing the resources, and their gifts, talents and abilities. Why? Because we are family! It pleases our Heavenly Father when His kids come home. Wouldn't you agree?

- There are so many more things that come from this process that you can't get in mere words. That is the EXPERIENCE, surprises, and little gifts, treasures and blessings that only God can provide. Those things are truly, ***"out of this world."*** Smiles.

So much fun! It is out of the fruit that you are holding a treasure in your hands. I pray for you, our dear reader that this book will help release you from the things that hold you back. I pray that this book will encourage your heart, and that you know God is speaking directly to you. I ask our Father, even now to send His peace and love over you and for you to know, that you know, you are loved.

In Jesus' precious name,

With love, Kathleen

Walking in Your Destiny

Moving Through the Fear

The Heart Goes On

Coralie J. Banks

I gripped my husband's arm, as the paramedics worked over him. His arm was growing cold and I realized, as if thinking through a fog, that he could die. Later, we found out his heart had actually stopped in the hospital.

The next weeks were a blur. I lived on a couch in the hospital family room on the cardiac ward, or at my husband's bed-side in intensive care. My husband had an operation and two stints put in, but the doctors warned us that he had a lot of heart muscle damage, and that we should prepare for heart failure.

How had this happened? We had no idea he was even sick, and now my dear husband, at only age 56, was at risk of dying. Or perhaps being an invalid. The man who came home from the hospital was grey, pinched and seemed suddenly aged. I sat up late every night reading medical articles on heart attacks and heart failure on the Internet, my own heart sinking as I read the grim statistics of how many patients would die in the first year after a heart attack.

I had the year previously started a new company, based on a dream and a vow to God, and I realized that it might not be possible to continue. I had just committed to producing a large volunteer-based community TV production in partnership with a church, and it had taken a lot of others' work and a lot of prayer to get it started. Teens, and their parents and grandparents as well as church members had devoted considerable time to preparing, but I was not sure if I should proceed.

I felt afraid, trapped and clenched into a little ball of fear and anger. Every night I cried out again and again "Why Lord? Please help us! What are we supposed to do now?"

I soldiered on with the project, but it was very tough going. Keeping 50 plus volunteers happy in a fledgling youth TV ministry was a large job, and it seemed impossible to keep everyone happy. In fact, I had several volunteers get quite nasty, and one even phoned me at home late one night wondering if I was a Christian as the script did not mention Jesus specifically (sadly, a requirement to be on community TV).

Meanwhile, my husband at home was very ill. He was sick and dizzy, and seemed very weak and listless. I checked in with him regularly, and had others do so too, but the fear and worry was never far from my mind.

I finally went to one of the pastors at the church and told him what was going on in my life, and with the program. His reaction was truly surprising—he smiled broadly, and said "Well, Coralie, you can sure tell that you are doing the right thing!" He continued, saying "WHENEVER we do anything worthwhile in ministry, there is always opposition." He went on to compliment me and the program, and to tell me to "stay the course," and that he and the ministry team "had my back" and would pray for us. He also asked permission to share this with some prayer teams.

He then shared a few stories, with no names, of things people have said to him over the years as he was about the Lord's work. Over time, these had become humorous to him, and we both laughed as he told the stories. It was a real relief to laugh.

Well, that was new thinking on several levels. Now that I had a shot in the arm from the dear pastor I started to look for words of help in scripture, and to ask others for help and regular prayer covering in specific ways.

Slowly, tentatively, I started to reach out to others for more mundane help too. Previously a fairly independent sort, I now asked others for recipes, to make food and arrange meetings for the project, and for help doing things like snow shovelling.

I also began to take it a bit easier on myself and others. I started to secretly see some humour in the inevitable conflicts different volunteering personalities tend to get in, and the perspective really helped.

Eventually, to my delight and surprise, we did get the program finished, and it was life changing for the families involved, award-winning, and was renewed by the network. I was so proud of it!

My husband improved greatly, and a new test showed his heart had been healed of damage. PRAISE GOD, and thanks to all the prayer warriors, many who I don't even know, that stood with us.

A scripture verse that really helped me is this: "For I know the plans I have for you," declares the Lord, "plans to prosper you and not to harm you, plans to give you hope and a future." NIV, Jeremiah 29:11

If I could go back, I would tell my former self these three things:

1. God is not surprised by what happened, and He has your future safe in His graceful hands. It will be okay, better than okay.
2. Reach out and ask for help and advice and prayer from others that have been there.
3. You will be able to help others because you will overcome this.

In fact, I have had so many positive changes in the two years since my husband's heart attack that it's hard to sum them up. My business has been blessed, I have been able to help others that are grieving and facing health issues, and the Lord has even allowed me to pray for people and see them miraculously healed before my eyes. I have a deeper and better relationship with Jesus, and am still growing. I have amazing ministry partners; Women of God that astound and delight me.

It didn't seem so when the journey started, but God had good plans indeed, and I am so glad that I held the course!

Coralie J. Banks is a film & TV Producer, media personality, author, speaker, editor, and strategist. Her award-winning growing company www.leapingcowgirl.com, focuses on strategic storytelling that SELLS! She is currently writing several books, including *Scary Technology, Privacy and Your Rights*, and *Yes You Can! Start a Successful Business After Age 45.*

Moving Through the Fear

Fear Not – Have Faith

Devi Boyle

I am the wife of a wonderful man and we have been married 19 years. I am also the mother of two beautiful, talented and delightful teenage girls. I moved from Guyana, South America at the age of 15 to Montreal, Quebec with my parents as they pursued a better life for their children in Canada.

Even though Guyana is a beautiful country, we often feared for our safety. In my teenage years crime was at a peak. This meant that we were not allowed to go to the movies after school or hang out with friends, but had to return home as soon as school was finished. It was shocking to find out that my friend stopped attending school because she was raped. Counsellors were unheard of, so victims did not receive the help that they needed. Even today, rape brings shame upon teenagers and their families as they have not been given any coping skills. Victims blame themselves and most would rather die than be raped. The suicide rate is extremely high as a result of this. Often there is no justice as these crimes are committed by people in prestigious positions.

Guyana is an English-speaking country. It is also known for its Anglo-Caribbean Cuisine, and various types of popular music include reggae, calypso, chutney, soca and many others. The national sport is cricket. Normally after work, the men spend their leisure time at the local "rum shop." It is sad to say that domestic violence and men cheating on their wives are very common.

Women are not always respected by men; they do not drive and are usually at home raising their children. It is very tough to make changes or fight for your rights if you are a female.

Growing up in Guyana was an interesting experience from a child's perspective. I was very secure in my Mother's love and I always knew that she would be there should we need her. She had four children by the time she was twenty-four, all two years apart. Mom stayed at home, however she wore many hats: she was our mother; our father; chief cook and bottle washer; not to mention our protector.

My father is a good man who struggled with a demon called alcoholism. Many times I begged him, "Daddy be strong, please stop drinking," but he seemed incapable of hearing what I had to say. My mother took charge and decided it was time to move us to be with the rest of her family who were in Montreal, as she did not see a future for her children in Guyana.

Mom left everything behind and moved us to Canada. We started all over again with nothing but a few dollars in our pockets. It was frightening leaving Guyana and moving to another country where we did not know anyone. Mom struggled to learn the Canadian way of life. My siblings and I grew up as a very close knit family. We did not ask Mom and Dad for anything, as we knew that our parents were working very hard to put us through school. Mom started to work outside of the house for the very first time!

I remembered being remarkably fearful of attending school, as I did not know anyone. It was a new school and we had to learn French, for we were in Montreal, Quebec. Since our parents were not born in Quebec we could not attend an English-speaking school.

No matter what I was up against, I never gave up hope. I turned it around by asking God to show me how to help others. I have never given up in believing in my heart that I can make a difference, make positive changes and to help to eradicate poverty. I have helped other non-profit organizations fundraise for a common cause, I have volunteered in teaching English as a second language to new immigrants, in turn giving to others, helping educate others and showing and teaching them that there is a better way.

I have taken the negatives and turned them into positives in my life. I remember very clearly when a person of influence said to me, "You cannot drive in this country!" Well, I took that as a personal challenge and proved him wrong two years later by getting my Canadian driver's license.

Through my experiences, I reflect back on my favourite scripture - Psalm 139: 13-14 ESV *For you formed my inward parts; you knitted me together in my mother's womb. I praise you, for I am fearfully and wonderfully made. Wonderful are your works; my soul knows it very well.*

I am secure in my Father's love and will put on the whole armour of God when I am called to do his bidding. God has a plan and a purpose for my life, but more importantly, God is not done with me yet.

If I knew then what I know now, I would leave myself with this advice:

1. Continue to seek and you will find even more. It is okay to be different and not follow others.
2. Be a leader, do not live in fear. Pave your own path and follow your heart.
3. If God is for us, none can be against us. No trial or tribulation can separate you from Christ.

Devi Boyle has a background with the Airline working as the pilot training coordinator for 15 years and is currently working as a small business manager. She is also working on her book called "Fight or Flight." Devi is very passionate about advocating for children who are being bullied in school. She plans to work with counsellors to educate other parents who are dealing with the remnants of the unrelenting and damaging effects of bullying of youth.

Walking in Your Destiny

Moving Through the Fear

Out of My Head and Into the Sky

Nicole Boyle

Envision this: You have been placed in the pilot seat. Picture being in full control of a machine that was constructed from metal and fabric, birthed to soar through the air like a bird stripped from the use of an engine. Feel the nervous excitement crawling under your skin when you reach thousands of feet above the ground and are told by a young instructor, "You are the pilot, make good decisions to get us on the ground safely." The reality

was: that was me. Only, I was 15 years old…
it was a week after my arrival to the summer
camp…and I was highly inexperienced.

I never thought it was possible to be afraid of
my passion. I had never foreseen that my
hobbies and dreams could be my undoing if I
allowed them to be. It was only on my 22nd
flight that my fear began to surface. That
important flight was my pre-solo check. Even
though I had been flying every day for
weeks, the reality of becoming a pilot never
quite sinks in until you are up in the aircraft,
alone. Flight 22 would determine whether I
was ready to fly by myself, and it had meant
more to me than anyone could understand.

Task saturation is a word used by pilots to
describe a situation where the pilot has too
many tasks that they are working on one at a
time, and as a result they miss important
information. This is very common in new
pilots. Questions are constant in the mind:
*Where am I positioned relative to the plane
in front of me? Where am I in relation to the
ground? Am I going too fast or slow? What is
my altitude? If the tow rope breaks, where
will I land?* On and on the list goes… which

is why students are taught to prepare first on the ground before flying the sky. The solution is to always be prepared. Preparation allows pilots to stay calm in emergency situations, because we have been familiarized with the problem once already.

Unfortunately, fear can still threaten to toy with you, and you can never fully prepare for every potential mishap.

My first pre-solo flight went approximately as follows: Excellent takeoff, great emergency simulation response, then, I felt for the first time that summer...sudden panic. I had lost my situational awareness, and blanked on my position relative to the map I had studied. I could not find the practice areas, my landmarks were a blur, my heart was skipping multiple beats. Complete fear grasped me, and I panicked. I allowed my fear to take hold of me, and I pulled the release knob. Keep in mind, I was flying with a standards pilot about twice my size that was extremely intimidating. The two of us were aiming to reach 2500' in order to complete all the tasks in the flight. Unfortunately, due to my task saturation, I created an unwanted fear that my body told me I needed to get rid of as fast as possible, creating panic and causing me to release from the tow plane at 1500'. At that moment I knew that I had failed the flight. My fear immediately dissipated, allowing me to collect myself. I was calm, I knew where I was, and I flew straight into the practice area and completed every upper-airwork task with ease.

This was the realization: I had been so focused inside my head that I forgot I was doing something I loved to do. My joy became a task, undermined by tests and grades and fear. This fear changed my love of flight into an obstacle that I then needed to overcome. I had two options: give up, or get up (literally, get up in the air!). I knew what I had to do. This flight caused me to re-evaluate my purpose of receiving my glider license. Isaiah 40:31 NIV says, *But they that wait upon the LORD shall renew their strength; they shall mount up with wings as eagles; they shall run, and not be weary; and they shall walk, and not be faint.* My faith in God was already strong, I knew that whatever I was doing would in some way aid me in the plan God has for my life. But what attracted me here? The answer became clear. I had decided to fly not only because it was a passion, but because I am able to feel closest to God when I am soaring with the birds. Flying was my escape from the world, a separate realm from every other existence.

Hopping out of the glider with a red-carded flight was one of the most blessed failures of my life. I planted myself in my passion to fly with a new purpose in mind: I was to work hard and enjoy every moment. I needed to get out of my head, escape all my negative thoughts, and completely commit to what I was doing.

If I had the option to have given myself advice before I left for the summer it would be this:

1. Know your purpose and the true attraction to your passions.
2. Do not allow the things you love to become obstacles in your life through fear. Enjoy each moment you have been given to the fullest.

3. Learn from your mistakes, take each stumble with a grain of salt and do not let fear or doubt seed in your judgement and cloud your mind.

Afterwards, the next flights were some of the easiest and most pleasant I had piloted. Each flight, after the red-carded flight, was completed with an exceeded standard mark. I passed my next pre-solo, felt the exhilarating reality of piloting during my solo, passed the Transport Canada written exam and received my wings. Passions must be pursued, a purpose must be found and fears must be triumphed over.

Nicole Boyle, currently a high school student in Calgary, Alberta, is pursuing a career in medicine. She has flourished in her passion for aviation, receiving her glider pilot's licence the summer of 2014 at age 16. In addition, she enjoys many other hobbies such as singing, playing various musical instruments, painting, instructing classes at her Air Cadet Squadron and wrestling for the Bishop Carroll Cardinals.

Moving Through the Fear

The Best Find I Ever Found

Margaret Buhler

I've had many fears facing me in my lifetime. For example, I have to get my rest in but there were so many things to attend and people to attend to. My eyes restricted me in reading. I would love to read into the night but that would prove to be a strict no-no. From childhood, reading and writing was my desire. Because of my eye-aches and headaches, I could not complete elementary school, let alone high school. I asked God: "Please, let me experience some Bible

School." The answer again was "No." Therefore, I fear the public. Let's face it – I am unschooled and ordinary.

Now, at 83 years of age, I was given the opportunity to attend Kathleen's Christian Writer's conference, "A Book is Never a Book." Not only was the travelling a concern, but also everything else involved created fear, which I had to overcome to a certain extent. To sit in a classroom with other high-ranking, schooled women using all the latest technology brought me fears which I had to learn to dismiss. People have used all the nice words of encouragement, such as "get up and go – for the Lord God is with you!" However, I was feeling "not so fast, not so easy." The closer it got to the conference event, I more I felt danger, threat, challenge and risk. For us older, land-loving settlers, it is a gripping and faith-raising life. Days of tears, triumph, fear and faith have been my fate – that is me.

I had to keep in mind that God will do whatever He wants to do – with or without me. I tried to make sure I did not lose touch with God, or my recognition of Him. God will find it possible either way. Was there wrestling? Yes, fiercely so. If I think something is God's will for my life, I take a step forward. So I started packing. I put out the fleece. But the answer was "No," I am not going. I unpacked. But then again, it seems there is a possibility. I began packing again. I must rely on God's faithfulness to light my way and point me in the right direction. I do not want to miss anything God is giving me in these twilight years of my life, but my age and declining health, sorry to say, seem to be against me.

What helped me through this whole ordeal was 1 Kings 17. This was God's word to Elijah in a time of famine – "Get away and hide by the Brook Cherith." God provided food and delivered it to his doorstep. The ravens would cater him. Ravens are very unclean birds. Elijah went and did according to the Word of the Lord. The ravens served the food according to the Word of the Lord. The food was okay but then the brook dried up. In verse 8, God came and spoke again. A Gentile woman was to cook for Elijah. However, she was about to run out of food, too. Elijah comforted her – "Do not fear, go and do." God provided for her, her son and Elijah. In verse 16, we are told the flour was not used up nor did the jar of oil run dry. This was all according to the Word of the Lord, Jehovah-Jireh, God Almighty!

The history of Elijah begins somewhat abruptly. He drops out of the clouds, so to speak, without mother and without descendant, which made some of the Jews think that he was an angel sent from heaven. But James 5:17 proves otherwise. My God Jehovah sends me and will own me and hear me out. We need not enquire whence men are, but what they are. Elijah tells us how he himself was taken care of in this famine. He was commanded to hide himself in Queen Jezebel's territory. God provided for Elijah by the most unused, insecure and unusual methods. Who can do these unusual things so perfectly with no problem? But Elijah had to obey. Had he not been there where God said, the ravens probably would have eaten the food themselves.

Trust and obey, hide and obey. We will be fed, blessed and protected in the most unexpected places. Be where God chooses you to be. For me, it is to hide quietly and be fed. My life is to be or live hidden and only come out when he bids me. Oh how he feeds me spiritually.

Some are made to be out in the public eye. My calling is not so, but privately to stay in tune with the Lord at home, where my work place is as is talked about in 2 Kings 5:9-11.

Why be anxious? What we may expect God to be to us: "I am the Almighty God!" He is a God that is enough, regardless of the situation. What God requires is that we should: "Walk before Me and be ye perfect". That upright walking with God is the condition of our interest in His all-sufficiency. All believers in every age should be looked upon as His spiritual seed. God sees the sincerity and seriousness of our return and repentance.

The vision of the sign "This is Jireha" was revealed to me Good Friday morning at 6:00 a.m. In my excitement I almost shouted out "This is Jehovah-Jireha." My sleep was over. I got up with a song in my heart and felt assured of His presence. No people, no scenery, only a brick wall with this sign. The Lord remembered me. He did. He presented me with a notice. "This is Jira." Yes, it is Jehovah-Jira. Jesus, is the best find I ever found.

Margaret Buhler lives in Winnipeg, Manitoba, Canada. She is a speaker, published author, skit writer and performer. She has a heart for young people, and taught Sunday school for years. She has been widowed for 16 years, and is the mother of 3 married children and has 7 beloved grandchildren. Margaret loves to cook, bake and share her wealth of goodies. She loves gardening.

Walking in Your Destiny

Moving Through the Fear

Listen to God's Voice

Sari Buhler

In 2004 I began to write a daily devotional from the book of Genesis for my family. I wanted to give them something to encourage them in their walk with Jesus. I chose Genesis because it was one of my favourite books from the Bible. It is a book of beginnings, full of history, failure, triumphs, and revelation of Who God is.

My family enjoyed the daily readings, giving me the courage to share them with a former pastor when he came for a visit. After reading what I had written up to that point, he encouraged me to continue and to look into getting my devotional published when I finished.

I was excited and shared that excitement with a Christian co-worker whom I liked and respected. At his request I let him read part of what I had finished. Even though I was nervous, I felt good about sharing this part of myself with him. I felt that I could trust him to be honest and fair in his evaluation of my material.

I was not prepared for his response. His words to me were negative, that I was using God's word to push my own agenda. What agenda? I could not understand what he meant, this devotional was not supposed to be about me. My spirit was crushed. I let his words seed doubt and fear into my heart. How could I finish something that wasn't sound, that wasn't putting God first? I stopped writing. I stopped trusting God to give me the words and wisdom that He wanted me to share with others and I put my devotional away.

In September of 2014 I met a woman named Kathleen Mailer at a *Living the Life You Dream* conference in Calgary. When you place your faith and trust in God He will always meet you where you are at, then He will take pleasure in leading you to places you never dreamed you would go or (as in my case) revisit. I know God has used Kathleen to minister to thousands before me but that day God brought me into her path to re-ignite a desire I had buried deep within, a desire to write. Shortly after meeting her I found the courage to pull out my uncompleted devotional and read it.

WOW, I wrote that? As I read through the pages, I was humbled by the words God had given me and I recognized that they were lessons from God. In setting the devotional aside, I had set God's words to me aside as well. Looking back, I don't know why I listened to my co-worker as I did. I let my fear of failure replace my faith in God to give me His words. However, my fear did not go away, it just shifted its focus in my life. What I had written was good, could I really do it again, would the remaining chapters be as good as the first ones? Once again I found myself doubting my ability to write. It took a couple of months for my heart to hear God gently remind me that He has not given up on me but will continue to give me the words and wisdom I need to finish my devotional.

My faith is built on God's word. Trusting the truths I have found in His word is essential to who I am. I know that when I share what I have learned from scriptures, I am sharing a small part of God with others.

I know I am not perfect but He reminds me from His word that *He who began a good work in you will carry it on to completion until the day of Christ Jesus* Phil 1:6 NIV

I have learned many things over the past several months but there are three that stand out to me:

1. Listen to my heart, after all, God speaks to my heart and His voice is more important than any other voice I may hear.
2. He brings the people we need into our lives at the exact time we need them most. He does this so He can fulfill His desires in us.

3. Don't give up; there will always be doubters and scoffers but if we focus on the desires God places in our hearts, He will give us everything we need to fulfill them.

Sari Buhler, a published author, holds a Missions diploma from Peace River Bible Institute. She has taught various Sunday school classes, served as a Sunday school superintendent, and has spoken to women's and youth groups.

Living Free Of My Shadows

Kay DaSilva

My brother once told me a quote by Ralph Waldo Emerson: "The moment you make a decision, the whole world conspires to make it happen." I remember repeating that sentence over and over to myself. Its profoundness had surely struck a chord in me. As a child growing up in Barbados, a small island in the Caribbean, my life choices were in the hands of my parents, as all kids' are. As I grew older, making decisions for myself was not something that came easy or naturally. I was known as the child who couldn't make a decision and it followed me for much of my youth and into my adult life. How many times in my life had I not made decisions when I should have, or left decisions for other people to make? Many! I think that I got used to it and eventually I believed it. Why would I decide when others would do it for me?

The lack of vision and confidence I had growing up became apparent early on. We are all shaped by our parents and our fundamental characteristics are passed on to us from them. As we grow, these characteristics either help us find and nurture the person we were meant to be or not. I didn't "find" myself for a long time.

The uncertainty of not knowing where I belonged and where I fit in followed me everywhere. Many shrugged it off as the mere normalness of who I was and no one questioned or challenged me to alter the course I was taking. This course was not one I could control because the decisions of every day "to dos" was out of my hands. I was led on one journey and destination after another because my parents married and divorced each other twice.

Through all of this travelling, I was lucky that I had my older sister and younger brother. Wherever one went, we all went. We were called the three musketeers. My poor sister became a "sparent" to us younger ones, a role that should never have been passed onto a twelve year old trying to find her own identity. As kids in all of this, where were we supposed to feel protected, secure or safe? I think all of this defined my unwillingness or inability to make decisions. They were just frivolously being made for me, for all three of us. It was however, what it was.

Because of all of the travelling, I can identify my childhood as based on the law of opposites. Five of us were pushing and pulling to live and find ourselves. We did, however, consecrate a bond that belonged to us no matter how weird it was. I believe there isn't a single family in the world that does not share this same excessiveness followed by happiness or ups and downs. It really does define the word family.

This was a course I took for the first 23 years of my life, which usually left me in a state of uncertainty, unsettledness, apprehension and emotional insecurity that I believe stagnated my ability to recognize my potential. But, my life was also filled with much love and good fun times. I did feel nurtured. But the invisible wall I had erected around me was to protect myself. With all the places we had lived, I don't think I was ever able to relinquish feelings of not being enough and never knowing enough.

It was not until I was 24 and able to live on my own and have my own space, that I began the process of finding me. I remember how excited I was to finally start making choices and decisions. Good or bad decisions, they were mine to make. It was a marvelous feeling! I had the power, the inspiration, the motivation and the drive to create my newfound independence. I also had the power to be a leader, a mentor and a source of inspiration to anyone who I became friends with.

It was many years later that I became brave enough to venture into a business relationship with my sister in a band celebrating the music of our heritage: Barbados. We had two CD releases in the span of five years, but somewhere along the way, something happened to our relationship that caused us to break apart, three times. The final time, I made the heavy decision to walk away because it was affecting my health, my emotional stability and my relationship with my husband.

Somehow through this loss, my eyes were opened to a belief that no matter what happens in your life at any given moment, something can drastically change, whether it be losing a family member or friend to death, or them being out of your life, divorce, health problems, and many more. The trick is to allow yourself to let it go and don't let whatever has hurt you, stop you. We must look to our own hearts. Yes, we all have paths with forks and if you choose "A" and if it is not right you can choose "B" at the next one. Trust your gut. Trust that you matter. Trust that no-one can derail you of these recognitions. It will only take one kind person or experience to trigger a shockwave of energy and support to catapult your life with purpose. This purpose will guide you to understand what you are meant to contribute to yourself, your family, your friends and to the world. The trick is to also recognize that it is those around you that are supportive and nurturing that will travel with you the longest.

I am reminded by a passage from the Bible from my childhood:

For you have been called to live in freedom, my brothers and sisters. But don't use your freedom to satisfy your sinful nature. Instead, use your freedom to serve one another in love. Galatians 5:13 (NLT*)*

Looking back, I wish I could have shared these truths with my younger kid-self:

1. Follow a path of living in a state of grace surrounded by positive attributes and mindset. It will teach you to "get back up" when life throws you down!
2. When your heart is calling you to do the best thing for yourself, listen to it!

3. Be willing to open your own doors and walk through them!

Kay DaSilva is an accomplished singer/songwriter/musician/musical theatre actress born in Barbados. She is an award-winning gardener, a published author and manages several investment properties with her husband. Her mission is to help others recapture their empowering selves that may have been misplaced in their journey through life.

Alone to Fulfill Our Destiny

Diane Gardner

My house guest, Ruth, came running out of her bedroom in a panic. "Diane, what's happening Why are you yelling 'I forgive you' and screaming 'no, don't do it' at Chuck? He's not here is he?"

She didn't know I was actually walking behind an open vision and not a live person.

She continued, "Are you OK? What's happening?"

I turned toward Ruth. "He's leaving! I had a vision of him leaving! He's really going to leave! He's not going to have a turnaround like we believed. I had a vision of him leaving and he looked at me with such hatred it was scary. Ruth, my heart feels like it's going to explode! I have to go pray, right now!"

I ran down the hall to my spare bedroom, where I fell on my face and sobbed uncontrollably in a way that felt like I would never stop. Ruth prayed for Chuck and me in her bedroom. As the uncontrollable grief subsided, I cried softly. The Comforter, Who is the Holy Spirit, comforted with the truth. He spoke a truth that broke my heart even further. Truth we don't want to hear may hurt more, but it also settles our hearts in a strange way because it's the answer.

I was terrified of what God would say to me about the full meaning of the vision.

I knew I needed to ask God some hard questions. I needed to gather the courage not to fear the answers, but accept whatever God said were the consequences of the vision.

"Lord, has Chuck already turned his heart completely away from me? Today you had our guest speaker, Dr. Valerie speak on moving into the next dimension, no matter what it costs. I'm going to move forward, even though I am afraid."

I came out of the room and shared with Ruth the essence of what the Lord revealed to me.

"Ruth, I asked a couple of really hard questions of the Lord. I asked, 'Father, the vision of Chuck leaving me is it permanent or temporary? Can I keep my marriage and fulfill your call and destiny for my life?' "

"The answer came back decisive and clear: *No, you cannot. So I am releasing you from the marriage because of Chuck's choices. His choices now are because of his choices over the years not to allow Me to heal his mind. Chuck has also refused healing from the root of bitterness from the beginning of your relationship. He has kept his anger toward his mother and your mother.*

When I unlock his pain, I bring it to the surface for healing. That's when he becomes angry, and instead of bringing his pain to

Me, he feels betrayed and doesn't trust anyone. During this time he allows the Enemy to manipulate the pain and cause him to isolate himself. Now he's convinced he can trust another woman and not trust you. He's going to accuse you of being abusive and untrustworthy.

Maintain your victory and talk openly when others mention these accusations. You cannot rebuke this storm or cancel its effect. You must go through this."

Ruth stared at me with wide-eyed amazement then said, "Please call a ministry friend and tell them about your vision. Maybe they can help you. I feel overwhelmed."

I made that call to a mentor friend and her husband whose board Chuck served on. They could not believe what was happening, and treated me like I was a hysterical wife that was overreacting.

When I thought about my own destiny I was reminded about the Scripture in Jeremiah.

For I know the thoughts that I think toward you, says the LORD, thoughts of peace and

not of evil, to give you a future and a hope.
Jeremiah 29:11 NKJV

After that fateful night I tried to let go of him in my heart because I had been consumed with praying for him. But after twenty-four years of marriage and seventeen years of ministry together, this was impossible without the Holy Spirit's help. How could I release him, Chuck, from my heart without building a wall of bitterness?

He moved out of our home, but we still worked together at the church for three more hard months. I had to overcome my fear of reprisal and gather the courage to ask him to leave. We could not continue with others thinking we were still together.

I wish I could have lovingly shared these three truths with myself:

1. When God calls you as a couple to serve Him together you are still only responsible for your part of the call. I was extremely afraid for Chuck's relationship (or lack of) with the Lord. Was he about to be judged? Looking

back I would've told myself to cast that care and move forward. I am not responsible for someone else's actions.

2. Don't presume that Chuck was going to have *one dream* or *one encounter* and suddenly become a different person. Have faith for God to move in his life, but don't put all your eggs in one basket. Believe that what you see is the real-deal and not just *temporary* insanity.

3. It's not your responsibility to either expose nor cover someone's bad behavior, even if he is your husband and pastor. Speak the truth in love without fear that you will get in trouble with the person that has the bad behavior.

Excerpt from *Overcoming the Enemy's Storms*, by Diane Gardner.

Diane Gardner is affectionately known as a "Grace Expert." She's the author of her riveting memoirs, *Overcoming the Enemy's Storms*. She holds Overcomer's Conferences.

Diane is a marketplace mentor/coach, chaplain, prison minister, and Advisory Board member with Christian Women in Media. She is the founder of Beautiful Women of God Seminars, www.beautifulwomenofGod.org

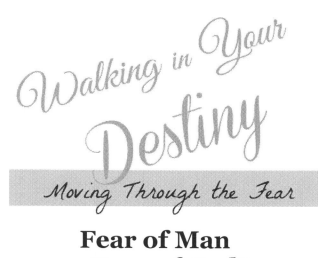

Moving Through the Fear

Fear of Man
or Fear of God?

Lorraine Jacyszyn

Has fear stopped you from fulfilling your
God-ordained purpose?

As a people pleaser, I realized that the fear of
what people might think was hindering me
from obeying God's leading. God was gently
teaching me to hear His voice by prompting
me to write poems to give to specific people.
Writing a poem was way outside of my

comfort zone. After all, I don't even like poetry. Going up to people I did not really know and giving them a poem seemed to me like social suicide. Unfortunately my reluctance to take these simple steps of obedience to God's prompting was causing me to become deaf to God's Spirit working in me.

After a time of feeling like my prayers were bouncing off the ceiling and complaining to God about why I wasn't seeing any fruit, I opened up the Bible to read John 14:15 *If you love me, keep my commands. NIV*

This scripture pierced my heart and I repented for being a rebellious child and not listening to my Father. I did not want to lose my relationship with God.

Then God showed me the parable of the seeds in the book of Mark:

*This is what the kingdom of God is like. A man scatters **seed** on the ground.*

*Night and day, whether he sleeps or gets up, the **seed** sprouts and grows, though he does not know how.* Mark 4:27-28

God is sovereign. It is His responsibility, not mine, to make the seed grow. My part was to obey and spread the seed. Now with a new mindset that it was up to God, I dutifully wrote whatever words He gave me. The next hurdle was giving these poems to people I was only briefly acquainted with. This required overcoming my natural shy and soft-spoken tendencies. Again through God's word He taught me to Love others and put them before my own fears.

For God has not given us a spirit of fear, but of power and of love and of a sound mind. 2 Timothy 1:7 *NKJV*

When I went with the attitude of serving others rather than worrying about what others thought of me it was a lot easier to step out and do it. Love overcomes fear.

Armed with a poem that God woke me up in the middle of the night to write, I approached the first person he assigned me to give a poem to. All I knew about this person was her name. Awkwardly I introduced myself and told her that God had asked me to write this poem for her. She read it and immediately broke into tears.

"I thought God had forgotten about me," she whispered. "How did you know that these are the exact words I needed to hear?"

God had used my hand to write the words to encourage this lovely woman and strengthen her faith. Seeing the stupendous result of being obedient to God's prompting, I continued one poem at a time, one person at a time. I rejoiced in the blessing of being a part of encouraging and strengthening others.

The other benefit as I took those first steps was that I could hear God's voice a lot clearer and recognize the Spirit's prompting. God started taking me to the next level. He knew I was deathly afraid of public speaking and to share a poem out loud to a group of people was utterly terrifying.

But in response to another scripture God gave me, *"When anxiety was great within me your consolation brought me joy. Ps 94:19 NIV*, I shared a poem in front of 200 people. My hands were shaking so badly I could hardly read the words. Even though my voice was quavering God used it to do his work and spoke to the people present.

Often I have to remind myself of the lessons learned:

1. Stepping out in faith faces the fear. Trusting God puts the onus on God to keep His part and puts my misperceptions into perspective. He gives me a new mindset.
2. Love over comes fear. Putting others first takes my focus off of myself.
3. Obedience brings me joy and takes me up to the next level of faith. The fear of God is way more rewarding then the fear of man.

I would still be in the same place if I had given into the fear of man. My mind and heart had hardened to the Spirit's prompting. If I selfishly hoarded the words that God gave me to encourage others, there would be a lot more unhappy people in this world and I would be one of them. Instead I chose to fear God over the fear of man. What will you choose?

Lorraine Jacyszyn is the mother of 12 wonderful children. She is a frequent contributor to *Today's Businesswoman Magazine*. Lorraine's poems have been published in various newsletters and magazines. She is the author of the soon to be released book: *Diapers, Desperation and Diplomas.*

Walking in Your Destiny

Moving Through the Fear

Natural Answers to Unspeakable Fear

Kathryn Johnson

I was so afraid for my daughter. Afraid that tonight might be the last night that she would be herself. She was hallucinating and crying. She was shaking and having violent involuntary muscle spasms in her head and neck. How could this have happened? She was only 7 years old. My mind wondered as I read my bible and the words there gave me hope to continue on.

He who is in me is greater than he who is in the world. 1 John 4:4 NKJV.

The night would be long, but my Father in Heaven would prevail.

My daughter was hoped for, prayed for and even desired. When she was born she was beautiful. She had rosy checks, curly brown hair and a robust cry. Although she had been exposed to drugs in utero she often amazed me with her immediate bond to our family and her willingness to love us despite the fact that we didn't meet until she was one day old.

Although she met all of her milestones within a typical time frame, she was slow at reaching them. She met each one just at the end of the typical time frame. When she finally did become ambulatory, she ran everywhere. She had a pitching arm that was outstanding. She could pitch a baby hot dog from her high chair to the sliding glass door hard enough for it to hit the door and bounce off. The high chair was at least ten feet from the door.

She easily became angry and would seem so frustrated when things didn't go her way. She often screamed and acted out physically. When she began to talk, her words were negative. Once she said to me, "You will be sorry that you adopted me, I will hurt you someday." I had never heard a child say something like that so once again I was scared.

My daughter's birth mom had Attention Deficit Hyperactivity Disorder or ADHD so we were certain that our daughter would too. ADHD runs in families because it is a genetic disorder. She also had depression, which we hoped our daughter would not inherit. Our daughter's birth mom was taking several anti-depressants when she became pregnant so we knew our daughter could be at greater risk of ADHD. We also knew that the birth mom had likely taken stimulant-type street drugs so we knew this could cause problems down the line. We felt that God had prepared us to care for this child. We also felt that our minimal knowledge of this illness as well as a whole lot of love could take care of any problems that arose.

As our daughter's hyperactivity increased and she began to grow, we decided that three and a half was a good age to determine if she did in fact have ADHD. She was officially diagnosed with ADHD and reactive attachment disorder. We decided to wait as long as we could to begin medication therapy, which we were told "is the best way to treat her illness."

At four and a half we began medication therapy. This went very well under the direction of her pediatrician. However, we moved and she had to be treated by a psychiatrist. I was upset that my little hyper girl was in the same office with people who were delusional and actively psychotic. However, we went and made the best of it. My daughter couldn't understand why the other patients were so different. We often stood outside to avoid any negative behavior on her part or on the part of the other patients.

When she was seven, everything fell apart. When we took her to the doctor he would increase the dose of our daughter's medication every time we said she wasn't improving. We asked for talk therapy and were told that psychology was a waste of time because it wasn't going to change the way her brain worked. We did as we were told, but were beginning to wonder if we were going in the right direction when an anti-psychotic drug was added to her long list of medications.

Everything came to a head when she began to have involuntary muscle movements in her head and neck. I was unsure if this was just another attention-getting behavior or if this was a real problem. Either seemed plausible at the time. I did make an appointment for her to see her psychiatrist, just to be safe. He diagnosed her with dystonia (a neurological movement disorder). He advised that we remove all medication immediately. We were to give her small amounts of an antihistamine only. That night I was more afraid than I had ever been. How could I help her? Her hallucinations were as if she had taken a drug like LSD. She was scared and clung to me all night. That was the first of many nights.

We made a decision to stop seeing the psychiatrist and continue using no medication. She lay on the floor kicking and screaming, hardly able to contain herself. We called out for help to our insurance. After a year they sent her to a neurologist. At that point she was given a different type of medication that made a big difference. The neurologist told us that some kids do better with a different type of medication. Our daughter was not one of those. We knew that even though things were not perfect, we were on the right path. Things were so much better, but we still struggled with issues of focus and control.

Sometime during the year that my daughter was off medication, while visiting a friend she asked if I had tried to change her to an organic diet. I was upset that my friend thought I was so ignorant. Although I was a licensed vocational nurse, I hadn't worked in about four years. I still remembered how the brain of an ADHD child worked and we had been taught that changing her diet wouldn't make a difference. How could an organic diet change anything?

I had grown up in a farming family. I didn't know of any reason to change our diet.

Organics was just a passing fad and it was expensive. I wasn't going to be a poor steward of what the Lord had given me. I thought to myself, "This girl must be out to lunch if she thinks she knows more than science."

After several months of continued problems, I was ready for a change. I had heard that removing gluten and dairy products had some good success for these kids. I attempted those changes without success. She remained the same. Finally, I decided to try an organic diet to see if it was helpful. In my heart I made this decision with the desire to say to all of my friends who had tried so hard to help that they were wrong. I thought that an organic diet was for nothing more than a bunch of old hippies with too much money to spend. I laughed in my heart because I too am an old hippie. How did I miss the bandwagon, I wondered?

The next week, I drove an hour from my little mountain town in search of organic food. I arrived at the store and realized that I didn't know how to determine which produce was organic and which was conventionally grown. If I was going to give my friends a fair chance, I had to find the right stuff. Finally I found a package of organic carrots. The only reason I knew it was organic was because the package said organic. I realized that I had a lot to learn if I was going to be fair to the challenge given by my friends and fair about the outcome with my daughter.

When I arrived back at home, I realized that the taste was far superior to conventionally grown carrots. So there it was, one for organic produce, and zero for conventional produce. As I enjoyed the taste of that wonderful carrot I thought to myself, "this is just a carrot, I am sure it won't work."

I would try to go every few weeks to purchase organic food and I learned to look closer and read better to find the prized organic food that would be the true test. It seemed to elude me. I couldn't find too much more than the carrots. Since my pastor in San Diego had this great saying "Do your best and commit the rest," I decided that was the best I could do. I felt I couldn't be fair to my daughter or my friends that way.

About eight months later, a friend told me about a group of farmers who wanted to bring an organic box of produce each week to our town. I asked "Is everything organic and certified?" I received positive answers to all of my questions, so I received my first organic box a week later.

What a difference that made! Although my daughter continues to use medication, there is a significant difference when she eats non-organic food. Food dyes are another problem that really makes a difference. She is now 15, and like most kids wants to eat pizza and burgers and fries. She has let me know, "I like these things, but they don't like me." We have worked with behavior modification and that has also made a huge difference. Her favorite time is family and hug time. I think that is just as important as the food changes.

With all of the changes, I have faith that we won't see her out of control or unable to control her behavior. On the worst days, she knows to use the skills she has learned to help her cope with the challenges of ADHD and depression. She is my special angel and I praise God for the opportunity to be a part of her life.

Although my fear was unspeakable, it was my faith in God that helped me get through all of those days, and my friends who humbly asked me to try a different path. I praise God for the Abundance of his garden. I praise God for our farmers who continue to grow organic healthy food and those that are willing to share with all of us.

If you have someone in your family who might benefit from a natural change you might want to consider these things:

1. Have an open mind about God's creation. *He causes the grass to grow for the cattle and herbs for the service of man.* Psalm 104:14 NKJV Many of the things that we need are a part of our world. Don't be so quick to find your answers in a pharmacy. Sometimes you do need that but take time to check out the natural too.

2. In Proverbs 27:17 NKJV it says: *As iron sharpens iron, so a man sharpens the countenance of his friend.* I spent so much time trying to prove my friends wrong. We could have been on the right path much sooner had I just listened to the kindness of a friend.

3. Realize that God has a plan for your life just as He does for my daughter. In Jeremiah 27:11 the Lord says to the children of Israel after they had been taken to Babylon by King Nebuchadnezzar *"For I know the plans I have for you,"* declares the Lord, *"plans to prosper you and not to harm you, plans to give you hope and a future."*

Kathryn Johnson is affectionately known to her Abundant Harvest Organics subscribers as "The Vegetable Lady." She is the Community Coordinator for the California Mountain, Desert and Northern San Diego Region for Abundant Harvest Organics. She is currently working on her new book, *From Farm to Table, Seed to Shining Seed.*

Walking in Your Destiny

Moving Through the Fear

Choose Faith Not Fear

Kathleen D. Mailer

"I am moving to Calgary when I am done high school to go to university. I have received a partial scholarship and I want to become a teacher. I think we should part as friends now since I will be so far away. If we are meant to be together after university then we can look at that too. I know it will be hard to be apart."

Looking into his eyes and saying those words was one of the hardest things I had done up to this point in my life. Thinking about this last year of high school as we dated, I realized that this boy had made an impact on me. He helped me to finally feel that I might be loveable to someone somewhere.

"Why do we have to break up? What is wrong with me? Did I do something wrong?" My heart broke as I looked into his eyes.

He was so confused and hurt over the fact that I would want to end our short relationship. I felt so bad! There was nothing wrong with him at all! I just knew in my heart that I needed to move forward in my life and walk into the next level of the my dreams – even if I didn't know what that meant exactly or how I was going to accomplish it.

My heart was crying out to me that I had to be strong and continue to live the call on my life. The darkness of fear began to seep through the crevices in my thoughts, taking root and branching out into every cell of my body. I could feel it choking me and causing me to doubt that this dream would ever happen.

The more we talked about my plan, the worse it got. Questions bounced around my mind like monkeys jumping from limb to limb. "Where are you going to live? How are you going to pay for the rest of your education? Who would be your friends? Would you be accepted? How will you find your way around the huge building? Will you get lost? What if you fail your classes?"

I finally conceded to stay in Saskatchewan. I ended up staying with my boyfriend and getting a job. I never used my scholarship, or even tried to go to university. I pushed through to do the best I could do and settled into a life in my small circle.

A very long 3 years later, I had the lesson of my life. The consequences of my "ill-fated" choice to walk the path that fear created verses the path that faith would create had come to a head.

I lay in my hospital bed crying out to God to cleanse me, save me, and help me. I asked for forgiveness for the life that I had led in the last few years that was far away from His perfect plan and will for my life.

I agonized over the last few weeks of events that took place that had brought me to my knees in this breaking point. The flashbacks were coming back to me at lightning speed... me telling my boyfriend, whom I was living with, that I was pregnant – then breaking up with him after I received his answer to my news...Throwing myself on my bed begging God to send me someone whom I could love and respect and that would love and respect me back... Getting my new job as a nanny, and then waking up on the floor in a pool of blood while the family was away... Me, ignoring the fact that I had a miscarriage and lost my baby... And now, at odds with myself in this hospital bed, alone, confused, scared, and more fearful of my future than ever.

The Lord then sent my friend Dan to find me. (Yes the same man who is not only my best friend but my husband of 23 years.) The Lord healed me, and my heart. He brought me back into his grace with love and tenderness.

He reminded me of the scripture, and the promise He gave me when I gave my life to him at 15 years old:

Seek the Kingdom of God above all else, and live righteously, and he will give you everything you need. Matthew 6:33 NLT

Looking back I wish I could have lovingly shared these truths with that 17 year old girl:

1. When God calls you, see it through and trust Him to bring your future into fruition.
2. Choose faith over fear every time. In the end you will save yourself AND other people in your life heartache and pain.
3. Don't let anyone try and stop you from listening to the direction that God is taking you. You can have council, yes, I am all for that. However, who is giving the council? What is their agenda? Is it aligned with the word of the Lord? In the honest answers of these questions you will find triumph over fear every time.

Kathleen D. Mailer is affectionately known around the world as the "International Business Evangelist." She is the Publisher of *Today's Businesswoman Magazine*; Founder (and) Facilitator of "A Book Is NEVER A Book" Boot Camp; and an author of 37 books including: *Prepare to Prosper, Taking Your Business To A Higher Level* www.PreparetoProsperBook.com, www.KathleenMailer.com

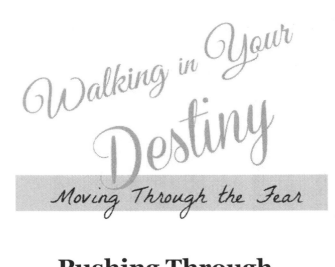

Walking in Your Destiny

Moving Through the Fear

Pushing Through

Darlene McIntosh

Today I was asked to write on the question, "Where has fear tried to stop you in the past?" Well first let me say that fear has controlled the better part of my life, for most of my life.

After becoming a born-again Christian, I am sure that I conquered a few fears. Notwithstanding, I still have a few strongholds in my life.

Finances has been an area of fear for me that has been hard to move through. I am afraid to make financial decisions and to seek greater independence financially. This is because I don't really feel or believe it can happen for me. I didn't get a good education, and because I stayed home looking after 5 kids, then became a single mom with no support, I got a late start in my career.

After leaving my abusive marriage, I started a restaurant in Northern BC. I started it because I thought at least then there would be food for the kids I kept with me. After some time, I wanted to return to Alberta to be near those of my children that I had to leave behind.

After my return I worked a restaurant, and then in a gallery. After the job at the gallery ended, I went to a seminar on money and fear about money. During the seminar, I had visions that I thought were from the Lord of me running a business, and I got excited and more brave again. I believed it would be possible to start my dream business. I loved art, and picture framing and so I started my own art gallery using the savings that I had from selling my house.

I was the only one working in the business, and I developed health issues and was really stressed and burned out. Eventually the business failed because I didn't have the energy to put into it, or enough money to back me up. In addition, I had to have three surgeries, and the stress and worry weighed heavily on me.

Once I recovered, I started hobby breeding dogs to make extra money. I had been training dogs as a hobby with my own pet and companion, a miniature Schnauzer named "Denver." Schnauzers remind me of little children and I felt I could learn to help the abused ones by watching how mother dogs reared their puppies.

Over the last six years I have grown the number of dogs I own, learned to groom very well, and taught myself in dog training. I often work with abused dogs, and I am told that I get amazing results in improving dog behaviour that others can't get.

I am considering writing a book because it would be something I love doing, and it would help dog owners. I have always wanted to write, but I thought that I had lost the ability after I got burned out.

When a Christian girlfriend prayed for me about my gifts, for the first time since I lost the gallery I felt life coming into my soul and my gut. I could tell that the Holy Spirit was calling me through her words to write.

I believe that the Lord can still use me. If He can use me to heal dogs when I can't speak their language, then He can still use me with words for people, in all my mess.

A scripture that comes to mind is: *I am come that they might have life, and that they might have it more abundantly.* John 10:10 KJV. I feel ready to give God, and to give me another chance by starting something new with Him.

Three things that I know will help me push through fear this time are:

1. Face your fear. I have to confess it and deal with it directly.

2. I have to attempt it and take a baby step. Even if I don't do it well at first, I have to try.

3. Prayer and support from the Book Boot Camp writing group is something I have never had before, and do this time. I believe that it will make a difference.

Darlene McIntosh is a dog trainer and breeder that lives in Red Deer Alberta. She enjoys art, antiques, decorating, planting an amazing garden, and loving all her "fur children." She loves to counsel, heal and motivate others.

Insanity

Margie McIntyre

Standing in my kitchen, I am in deep thought, with a frustrating battle raging in my mind. I haven't been spoken to for a least two days and as always, I have exhausted myself again and again with apologies, trying to solve our marital problems and always trying to figure out how to be a better wife. It is impossible to please him when he is in this state. I know that when he comes through this and he's nice again, he's actually an awesome guy!

It is so confusing! I'm not exactly sure how we even got to this place, yet again. It appears that he thinks he is punishing me because I haven't done things the way he wants them to be done or said things the way he thinks they should be said. Why do I have to think his way or say things the way he wants me to say them? I'm capable of thinking for myself and should be allowed to - shouldn't I? What is wrong here and how can I fix it? There just doesn't seem to be an answer.

I asked God, "What do I do?"

What happened next took me completely by surprise! Although I didn't hear the actual words, a voice spoke clearly in my head, "Give him to Me!" I knew exactly what God was saying to me. There was no mistaking Who was speaking - it was clear.

Experiencing incredible relief, I immediately realized that was my only answer. "Really Lord, I can give him to You? You'll take care of him and You'll take care of me?"

I knew His answer was "Yes" - so I did it. Right there I did it! An incredible sense of peace came over me and I knew I was on a new path.

Little did I realize that step of faith, that new path, was going to be a scary one! The withdrawal continued for another two days and when I felt the least bit tempted to address his silence and try to fix it, the words "Give him to Me" came back immediately. That settled me. I wholeheartedly gave him up to the Lord.....He could deal with him.

The next day was Christmas and his behavior changed because we had family over. He wasn't about to expose that side of himself to them. Consequently, the next few days were actually quite pleasant - he seemed to have forgotten his frustration with me.

It was only a few days later the hammer came down once again. I disagreed with him. The way I thought about something was not the way he wanted me to think about it and he was angry, so angry..... I just left for work.

Within a couple of hours I received a text saying that this time he had had enough. I had better come and get my belongings before eight o'clock that night, as the doors would be locked and I would not be allowed in. He felt we needed to separate for a time, giving me a chance to think about what I really wanted in this relationship.

I wasn't overly surprised, just extremely frustrated, because this had happened so many times before. I had told him every other time that he couldn't kick me out, because the house was half mine and as long as I acted like nothing had happened, he would settle down and act normal again.

This time was different though. God was at work! I realized that I couldn't keep doing the same thing over and over again and expect different results. That is the definition of insanity - which was exactly what was going on - insanity! Something had to change!

I spoke to my adult son who knew of our situation and he suggested I go to the Women's Shelter to ask for some guidance -

to see if they could help me understand what was going on in my relationship. It seemed a sensible option, so off I went.

I was introduced to a counsellor who took some time with me, asking questions and assessing my situation. Question after question I responded to with a "yes." Slowly... it dawned on me! "Oh no...... I'm in an abusive relationship! Me? ...Really? ... No! ...Yes! ...Really?" I was in shock - absolutely stunned! I had never even considered abuse as the issue. Never even gave it a thought!

When she read the "Cycle of Abuse" to me, I could have inserted his name right into it - he fit the description to a T! Wow....You could have knocked me over with a feather!

Now what?

She told me that I was in a "classic verbally abusive relationship" and that I had every right to stay at the shelter for a month until I found another place to stay or I chose to go back home.

Fear gripped me! What if I left him? What would he do? What would I do? Would I be able to support myself? Should I leave, would that be the right thing to do? Would I be leaving for good? Surely he would change if he knew I meant business and then I would be able to go back home? What if he didn't?

I asked the counsellor if I could have a couple of hours to think about it and she told me to take my time. I left her office completely stunned and shaken to the core!

Fear had taken over. If I left him, I would be leaving all my financial stability. I am 64 years old.... I would have no home. If I went to the shelter, where would I go after that? The truth was that I didn't really have any security with him anyway. He was always holding finances over my head and his controlling behaviors and manipulative ways had me on a roller coaster ride, as it was! Maybe leaving really would be the best for both of us. Then I remembered God had said, "Give him to Me."

I wouldn't be able to fix anything - that was God's job.

My destiny was a matter of the choice I was about to make. Would I break through my fear of my loss of so-called security and break the cycle of abuse or would I go back home and pretend nothing had happened as I had always done... and continue the cycle?

I made my choice! Two hours later I drove up to the Women's Shelter with my things and signed in for a two week stay. This step of faith to break through my fear has changed my future for the better.

It is not easy, but it is worth it to have my sanity back, to be able to think clearly once again and to take control of my own life.

Now I live in the basement of a friend, who has reached out to me in my time of need. I am in the process of moving forward in my life, receiving the counseling I need to become emotionally healthy and learn the truths about myself that got me into yet another abusive relationship. I am open to reconciliation but there will be conditions attached. If he will recognize his hurtful, controlling and manipulative behaviors and if he will surrender himself to the Lord to make the necessary changes in his life, maybe our relationship could work.

I now understand that I am not the problem, the abuser is and he must recognize his problem before we can move ahead together. That is.... if he will. It is up to him. I cannot fix him - only God can. He is the one who broke the commitment in our marriage relationship many times over with his abusive behaviors of, one day loving me and hating me the next. I am not in the wrong to be separated from him, it will be up to him to recommit his faithfulness to me. I understand that now.

I have been encouraged through this time by one of my favorite scriptures:

Rom 8:28 *And we know that in all things God works for the good of those who love him, who have been called according to his purpose.*

I am reminded of the fact that this is not all about me, and that there is a much bigger picture here. God never wastes a hurt and he is not finished with me yet!

As I move forward on this journey, I have learned and will hold fast to these truths:

1. I will believe that God really does know what He is doing.

2. I will make sure I continue to have a very solid support group comprised of friends and professionals who truly know the Lord and care about my welfare.

3. During the separation I will not get caught up in <u>any</u> form of communication with him. He must not have any opportunity to control or manipulate me. When he shows his counselor, who is also in communication with me, that he is taking full responsibility for his behaviors, and is no longer blaming others, only then will we be able to consider the possibility of renewing the relationship.

It has been pointed out to me that reconciliation can only come out of complete separation.

Reconciliation with Christ can only happen once we realize we are separated from Him.

Margie McIntyre works as an advisor, helping families manage their financial futures. She is also the inspirational author of *Mind Matters - Change Your Mind, Change Your Life!* She uses real life story-telling to demonstrate and teach us about the importance of our minds.
www.mindmattersseries.com

Moving Through the Fear

Trust Like You've Never Trusted Before

Linda A. Olson

As I scanned through my multitude of e-mails, three little videos caught my attention. They focused on Kathleen's boot camp; "A Book is Never a Book". I had been to many Christian Writer's conferences but never heard anything like this. The part that was always missing for me was the marketing piece.

I knew I needed to attend the conference but it seemed impossible. It was a week later, and my 24-year old business had gone bankrupt. Before going to bed, I quietly prayed and asked God to show me if this was really from Him or just something I thought would be fun to do.

In the morning I briefly spoke to my husband and much to my surprise he was quite supportive as long as I could work out the expenses. I called my credit card company to see if I had possibly accumulated enough airline points for my flight. Much to my surprise not only did I have enough air miles but also there was a direct flight available. This was almost unheard of so close to the date of travel. I clearly knew it was no coincidence. God was in it. Then I spoke to my husband about using some of our points if I could find a hotel within a reasonable distance from the conference. He agreed. After several calls I found a great hotel just a mile from the conference that would take my points. It was another confirmation. After getting onto Kathleen's website I discovered that she still had the early bird pricing on and it included lunch. Wow, I could hardly believe it. Now the out-of-pocket expenses were reduced to a minimum and I knew I could go. Everything was a green light. By noon, I had everything booked and my registration was complete. Kathleen returned my call and said she and her husband were in heavy prayer asking God to bring just the people He wanted to the conference. Mine was the first call. It was the final confirmation. I felt like it was a big test of my faith and I passed with flying colors. (That alone, was miraculous.) All I knew is that God must have something extra special for me to clear the path and open all the doors. It was amazing!

I soon discovered this was just the preliminary test. Halfway through the conference, Kathleen unveiled her six-month Bestseller program. I believed in my heart this was for me but now I was really overwhelmed. I didn't even have the money to get to the conference, how could I possibly pay for this program with no income? Besides, I didn't have a clue what I was going to write about so why was this even important for me to sign up for?

As Kathleen closed in prayer she walked throughout the group to see if there was someone that needed prayer or a word of encouragement. I felt safe near the back of the room, confident that I could hide my struggle. As she came near, she put her arms around my shoulders and simply said, *"Some of us are overwhelmed with fear."* As soon as she named the enemy, FEAR, the tears immediately surfaced. Fear had been identified. I knew I felt overwhelmed but had not been able to identify that I was experiencing fear. Now I knew whom I was dealing with. But did I have the courage to drive out the enemy and would I clearly hear God's voice?

I had often quoted a verse found in 2 Timothy 1:7, *"For God has not given us the spirit of fear, but of power and of love and of a sound mind."* I got the first part – fear is not from God. But could I grasp that I had direct access to His power, His love and His sound mind?

All I knew is that I was facing an even bigger challenge. If satan was attempting to keep me from what God had for me, could I trust God to provide? In my hotel room, I poured out my struggle to God. Then, He reminded me of a word I received earlier in the year that said, *"This is the year to trust Him like you have never trusted Him before."* Less than a week ago, God had miraculously provided for me to get to the conference when it seemed impossible, why was it so hard to trust Him now?

As I called my husband, he wisely confirmed, *"This is not about the money. If this is what God wants you to do, then we have to trust Him to provide."* I knew that in my head but could I believe it in my heart? Before we hung up, my husband prayed with me and I humbly confirmed that I would follow through what I knew I needed to do. It was an act of obedience. My heart was at peace and I slept soundly.

The next morning in the shower, five or six book titles came to mind. I could hardly wait to get to the conference to see what God had for me now. At the first opportunity I filled out the paperwork to confirm my decision to do the Bestseller program. Paying for the conference was no longer my struggle.

Instead, I was excited to see how God was going to come through. Before the day was done, I had my title, a rough outline and was ready to go forward. It had been a huge breakthrough.

As I got to the airport, I could hardly wait to get to my seat and begin writing. By the time my flight landed in Los Angeles, I had a good portion of my book written. Then, I discovered that was the easy part. What I didn't know was the challenge that lay ahead following through with every step of the marketing. In one of the steps, Kathleen challenged each of us to pre-sell at least 100 books before it even went to print. All I knew was that I didn't even know how to sell my previous book when I had it in my hand, much less when I didn't have it in my hand. If this was going to happen, it would definitely be a God thing.

Together with the new skill of marketing that I was learning and the skill of speaking that I had learned earlier, I knew exactly what to do. I planned several gatherings and much to my disappointment only a few people showed up. What surprised me most was that even with only three people I would sell nine books. My sales were as much as 300% when the average sales are often less than 10%. Once again, God confirmed that He was doing a new thing. He was there for every step of the process. Within a short time, I had sold 125 books before my book even went to print. Less than six months later printed on the front cover of my book was #1 Amazon Bestseller.

My heart was full and overflowing. I could hardly believe what had just happened. And then, I realized, this was just the immediate fruit. God was up to something much bigger. During this process, Kathleen and I had connected in a way that was something only God could do. There was an immediate bond and trust. As we experienced each other's gifting, skills and character, and shared several platforms together, we were in awe with the unity of our hearts. Kathleen's desire to train Christian authors and my desire to train Christian speakers were a perfect complement to each other. I invited Kathleen to come to Southern California and she confirmed that God had already laid that on her heart. After much planning her and Dan joined us for a few weeks of intensive ministry laying the groundwork of what is yet to come. Then she began opening up doors for me in Canada. We have no idea where all of this will take us but we know it is more than we imagined!

As I reflected on the past year of my journey, I discovered it was only as I took my eyes off my circumstances (storm) and focused on Jesus (walking on the waves), that I, too could walk on water. None of it would be possible without the extra measure of faith. I realized that when the enemy (fear) was identified, he lost his grip. I had access to God's power and as I humbly submitted to Him, and resisted the devil, (by quoting and believing 2 Timothy 1:7) he fled just like James talks about. I needed to commit to God first before I could clearly hear His voice and see His provision. God was stretching me to take me to a higher level. He wanted to give me a promotion that could only come by way of faith.

Lord, help me to remember that the purpose of the storm is to trust You like I've never trusted You before.

Linda A Olson, Palmdale, California. Linda is the Founder & CEO of *Made for Something More*; Creator & Facilitator of the *Unstoppable Blessings* coaching program; and Creator of the *Christian Speakers Get Paid* Speaker Training program; International speaker & author of several books including *Uncovering the Champion Within, 101 Truths to a Powerful You.*

Moving Through the Fear

Overcoming the Voice
of Fear

Adriana Perez

I was sitting in the airport awaiting my layover flight to the publishing conference that I knew it would undoubtedly change my life forever. For the past three weeks my heart was nearly bursting, I was so overcome with excitement at everything I would learn. I would finally reach my dream to become a writer.

And yet, just hours away from the event I had been looking forward to for weeks, I felt uneasy. I felt my fear and apprehension battling with me, and I heard the thought, "You're tired and cramping, what good are you like this? Just leave right now. Don't you want to go rest at home? Don't you hear the flight back to San Diego calling you?" And I did.

During that 4-hour wait between flights, as I continually heard "San Diego" being announced over the intercom, I suddenly wanted nothing more than to be home. I felt homesick, and I wanted to return to the ones I felt comfortable with instead of strangers in a strange town. I found myself wondering at the possibility of changing my flight right then, and then the fear gripped me tighter, as if it was saying, "Yes. Yes, that's it!"

Instead, I called my "angel on earth," my mom. When I had first heard about the life-changing event, I instantly wanted to attend but I told myself that since I couldn't afford it, I would attend the following year. But my mom firmly said, "No. You are going to this." At the start I didn't have enough money for the registration fee, let alone for international traveling expenses. But my mom declared it, and miracles came into my life so completely that in just one week I had everything I needed to attend the event.

It was my mom who brought in all of the connections and assistance, but through her, I could no longer deny that God was showing me that He also declared I would attend, and that He was providing my every need to do so. Through witnessing His miracles in my life during that week, my faith grew. I learned how powerful His love was for me, and that by just abiding in His love, all my needs and desires would be met. Not only that, but that He was going above and beyond any expectations that I could have ever previously imagined.

As I got ready for the conference, I found myself battling negative thoughts regularly, but I was still full of so much excitement that I was able to brush it off. But sitting there in the airport, alone and away from everything and everyone I loved, I felt the fear trying to take hold of me. When I felt it overwhelming me, without really thinking, I picked up my phone.

"Hi, Mom," I said, and we began to chat about the day and things that were going on. She was busy, and usually I would let her go and call her back later, but in that moment I felt a need to stay on the line, so I pressed on with the conversation. When we began talking about the event I was traveling to attend, she said, "Just know that you're not going there to create yourself. This is the most important thing--"

And then the line went dead.

When I tried calling her back, the call would not go through. I tried over and over until I finally looked at my phone in bewilderment, and I prayed, "God, if I am to hear this message, please let this call go through!" In the exact moment I finished the thought, the call went through. We expressed our confusion and relief, and then she continued with her advice: "The most important thing to remember, Hija, is that everything you need is already inside of you."

This thought struck me, and in my heart I knew that what she said was true. She gave one last piece of advice before we said our goodbyes: "Write down what I just told you."

We hung up, and I began to write out the quote. In writing it, all of a sudden all of the scripture and life lessons and events that had happened up until that point fell neatly into place, and told me a story: Just as our physical DNA is complete at the moment of our conception, so is our spiritual DNA. The seeds of our purpose have already been planted in us from the start, and it is our job to care for and nurture ourselves so that these seeds will have the opportunity to burst forth and blossom in our lives. And just like that, my first book was revealed to me!

I was reminded of the scripture I had recently sent to a friend who was struggling with coming into her power:

For God gave us not a spirit of fearfulness; but of power and love and discipline. 2Timothy 1:7 (ASV)

The weight of the message settled into my heart and spoke to me. The whole experience made me see how close I had come to allowing my fears to keep me from finally realizing my dreams. I realized that God has given us three powerful tools to overcome our fears themselves:

1. God gives us His power, and when we pray and allow Him to work through us, His power breaks all chains.
2. Love overcomes all sins, and interrupts the process of doubt, worry, and any other fear that tries to hold us back.
3. God teaches us knowledge through scripture, which can be continually referenced in order to dispel any fears that might be trying to take root in us.

With these three keys we can continually weed out what does not serve our purpose, so that the seeds of God might have the room and nourishment to grow into fulfillment.

Adriana Perez is a published author and will soon be releasing titles such as "Tending Your Inner Garden: Keeping the Soil Rich" and "Illuminated: Glowing for God". Her goal is to assist others in discovering their purpose through self-expression in all of its creative forms, thus spreading Light into the world one heart at a time.

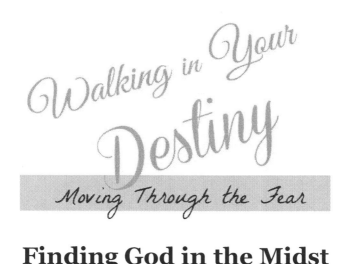

Walking in Your Destiny

Moving Through the Fear

Finding God in the Midst

Kristine E. Riley

I curled up on the couch pulling the blanket close around me. I was in pain physically and emotionally.

The tears came, slowly at first, then in a torrent.

"God, what is happening?" I cried out.

It was February 2010.

Like a movie in reverse, my thoughts drifted back a short four years ago. 2006. My life and the second marriage I had known for 25 years had unraveled; the authorities imposing a restraining order removing my husband from our home and my life.

The emotional pain was doubled as this was my second marriage. (My first marriage fell apart after seven years.) I found myself on my own with our two children. Gone were the hopes and dreams of my husband and I growing old together surrounded by children and grandchildren.

Now my life's movie rolled ahead.

Over those years from 2006 - 2010, God had begun healing me from the inside out. He reached back, far into my childhood, to the times I was molested during those tender, young years.

He showed me how my trust and the healthy boundaries to keep me safe had been broken - not once, not twice, but three times.

The tools I needed to prepare for marriage and enjoy and thrive in a healthy marriage were missing or broken.

Now I began to understand. The understanding brought healing and, with the healing, forgiveness which came not only for others, but for myself. It gave me the voice I have today to break the decades-long silence about abuse - in all its forms.

We know that time and life move forward, whether we are ready and willing, or not.

At the end of 2006, I heard God speak clearly to my heart, "I Am calling you out." "Calling me out, Lord?" I asked. "Can you tell me more?" … Silence.

In January 2007, God spoke to my heart again. "I Am calling you out." This time I didn't ask. I tucked His Word in my heart - and waited.

March arrived and, with that, God spoke once more to my heart. "You are called out." My heart was so touched, so moved, that I answered Him with the words of Isaiah echoing in my heart. I responded, "Here I am. Send me."

And, with that, he began to close the doors to the ministries I was involved in and, at the same moment, began to open doors to the new city He was sending me to.

Was this emotional? Yes! I was excited, sad, fearful, and full of faith all in the same basket.

The British Columbia coast was where I had been born and raised. It was where I had spent the last 50 + years of my life and, where I expected to retire.

But my plans were changed. My plans were exchanged for God's plans.

For me, this was a definite "stepping out of the boat" moment!!!

But over and over, God confirmed each step, allowing me to be sad for those I was leaving - family, long-time friends, the "security" I thought I had built around me.

I was leaving a grandson, whom I was very close to. I tried to explain that God had a job for me to do. My grandson tried to understand as much as he could. Later that night, I wept as if the tears would never stop.

God, in His infinite wisdom and love, spoke ever so gently to me, "Don't you think that I Am able to look after him?" All I could do was to say, "Yes, Lord, You are able to look after him."

How do you leave the job you have had for almost 25 years? How do you leave the people you have worked with who have become like family? You have shared the eventful moments of their lives - marriage, the birth of children and grandchildren, the joys and sorrows of life.

One morning, as I opened up the office and stepped through the door, I stopped. I looked around. Something had changed. It was puzzling. I looked at the furniture, which still was in the same place. Nothing in the office had changed.

Suddenly God opened my eyes and I said, "Oh, this isn't my office anymore."

As God continued to put the pieces together, April 2008 arrived. Along with the moving truck and my car full of boxes, I arrived at my destination.

People say that God works in all the details of our lives. That proved to be very true. Even the moving boxes had been thought of. A lady, who had recently moved to my town from the city I was going to, gave me her moving boxes.

But now, ever since I arrived, everything seemed to be going sideways.

The job that had been waiting for me when I arrived in April suddenly closed in October of that same year due to a declining market.

But - God provided!

In early 2009, I was hired as an administrative assistant for a busy office. Yay God! I was jumping up and down thanking Him. But, on the last jump, God spoke yet again to my heart that this job was only for a season. I wondered, "What does that mean?"

By the end of 2009 and into the first few months of 2010, I was undergoing medical tests for the intense pain in my body.

And now, a fresh batch of tears fell. I knew that I was not to move back to the town I had left. But, what now?

"God, do You still have a plan for me?" I whispered through the tears. In that moment, I felt His love wash over me, and all I could do was - cry.

In the middle of that very night, God woke me up. He began to share a story from His heart. I hastily grabbed paper and a pen and began to write.

It was a book for children. The title was to be, "The Story of Henrietta Caterpillar." He showed me what "Henrietta" would look like and where the illustrations were to fit in.

Within four hours the story was on paper and re-written on the computer. Then I waited.

In June of 2010, I took a trip back to see family and friends.

As it happened, another friend I had not seen for a long time was visiting friends in the same area.

"What have you been up to?" she inquired. She followed this question with another. "Do you do any creative work?"

I paused and then replied, "Oh, I wrote a book." We discussed the story, and then my friend asked, "Do you have a publisher?"

When I said that I didn't, she said that she knew Kathleen Mailer who owned "Aurora Publishing" in Calgary. She said, "I'll help you get in touch with her."

The day arrived and Kathleen and I connected. She was so enthusiastic about "Henrietta," which made me even more excited about this little book with a BIG message.

Kathleen went over every detail of the publishing process, and scheduled another phone call after I had time to think and to pray about it.

One afternoon, around 3:00, I began to pray about "Henrietta," finances, anything - and everything. At 3:20 my telephone rang. It was Kathleen. She said that she had arrived home from work, thinking she should call me immediately rather than in a couple of days.

Kathleen asked me if I had had time to think about the next step. I hesitated - I was so afraid. I was out of work, didn't know if or when I could return. Not one word came out - fear had literally paralyzed me.

Kathleen reassured me it was okay, and we could leave it for now.

Then, something rose up inside me, and I said to Kathleen, "I do not want to get to the end of my life knowing God has something for me to do, and I did not do it. It would be the biggest regret of my life. Yes! Let's do it!"

That day, faith rose up and pushed fear aside. Faith overcame fear.

And the rest, they say is history or as I have learned, "His-story".

Many years before, God had placed in my heart that, one day, I would go to Africa. I had kept that dream in my heart, not knowing how that would ever come to pass. And now, from that decision to see "Henrietta" come to life, came the fulfillment of my first mission trip to Africa in 2011- with "The Story of Henrietta Caterpillar" to read to the children there to inspire and encourage them with hope.

The Scripture which God gave me as the foundation for "The Story of Henrietta Caterpillar" was Jeremiah 29:11 NIV: *"For I know the plans I have for you"*, declares the *Lord, "plans to prosper you and not to harm you, plans to give you hope and a future."* And this has become my foundation Scripture too.

Finding God in the Midst....God moves you from fear to faith.

"Faith sees the invisible, believes the unbelievable, and receives the impossible."

Corrie Ten Boom

Kristine E. Riley is the published author of children's books and short stories. Her successful children's series, "Henrietta Caterpillar" now finds a home in many countries in the world. Soon to be published is the first book in her new series, "Finding God in the Midst....My Journey from Fear to Faith."

E-mail:kris.byheavensdesign@gmail.com
Website: www.byheavensdesign.com

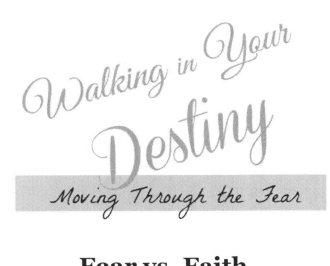

Moving Through the Fear

Fear vs. Faith

Barb Tatlock

"I have a nebulous grey feeling that you are not the right person for the job."

Those were the words that one of my bosses used to tell me that I was fired in a group meeting of my co-workers. I sat there, stunned. All sorts of thoughts were running through my head, but I couldn't actually speak because I knew I would say too much or not enough, and how do you argue against "nebulous grey" anyway?

Let me give you some background to this story. Five months previously I had returned from a Discipleship Training School with "Youth with a Mission." I had gotten this job, at a very "new age" office, with the quiet codicil that I shut up about my faith. That should have been a hint, but really, was I going to go around spouting Jesus all over the place? I don't think so! I believe God was trying to tell me, even then, that I needed to set down my own self-sufficiency and rely totally on His all-sufficiency but my fear wouldn't let me. I needed a job, and wasn't this a job? God hadn't done such a great job of finding me a job, so I obviously needed to find my own.

From that day forth I was under the microscope. If I was a minute late back from lunch, it was commented on. If Bill, one of my bosses, didn't see me working where he thought I should be, it was commented on. Never mind the fact that I was at someone else's desk doing their job because they were out sick. So needless to say I felt like I was walking on eggshells, and I was.

My three month review had passed without comment so I kind of thought I was safe, but God had other plans. Two months later we were in a staff meeting when Bill dropped his bombshell. His nebulous grey feelings comment shot right to the heart of my insecurity and fear of being rejected and without a job. However, this was not the job that God had for me so He ended it.

About 15 minutes after the meeting ended I found Bill in his back office and asked if I could talk to him for a moment; he looked very uncomfortable but finally said "Yes." God allowed me the opportunity to express to Bill that I recognized that this business was his dream, not mine, and that to me it was merely a job. A job I liked, but really it was still just a job. And I told him "that truth be told, this is not my passion, so maybe that is where your nebulous grey feeling is coming from."

Sounds all very mature and grown up, doesn't it? Until I got down to my car, which I had just bought and now had no way to pay for. As I was sitting in my car, wailing like a baby, the Lord very clearly said to me: *Have*

I not commanded you? Be strong and courageous! Do not tremble or be dismayed, for the Lord your God is with you wherever you go. Joshua 1:9 NASB

Wow, that was a wake- up call! So to my 32 year old self I would compassionately say:

1. Trust God to find you your job; do not rely on your own wisdom.

2. When something depends upon you being quiet about your faith, no matter what, RUN!

3. No matter the circumstance, know that God has your back! Don't let fear dictate what you will or will not do.

Barb Tatlock is an author with a heart to heal the broken-hearted. Her heart's longing is to see people walking in the fullness of who God has called and created them to be.

BOOKED!

Is Kathleen available to speak at your next big event?

Find out now by connecting to our website:

www.KathleenMailer.com

Made in the USA
Charleston, SC
28 April 2015